Actin *Monolo____ ___ ___ ____*

Volume 2

More Original Monologues and Scenes For Kids 7 to 13, and -- a section of 'Shorty' Warm-Up Scenes

by Bo Kane

"Acting Scenes & Monologues For Kids! Vol. 2"
Published August, 2017
Burbank Publishing
212 S. Reese Pl.
Burbank, California 91506
Burbankpublishing@gmail.com

ISBN 0-9841950-4-1

Written, published, and printed in the United States.

Cover - Film Strip: Tyler/Tony, Ari/Marley, Nick/ Mylo/Tiber, Isa/Kendra, Jett/Raquel, Trevor/Austin, Ruben, Kaden/Sara, Scarlett/Dylan/Eddie.
Group: Sara, Jude, Samantha, Lucas, Scarlett, Ayon, Bo, Eddie, Aristotle, Aiden, Tiber.

Book Cover and masks design by *Thomas Cain*

Monologues

Scenes - Two Kids

* 2 girls and 1 boy

Scenes – Kid and Adult

"Shorty" Scenes *just a few lines each*

Foreword

Congratulations! You made it to Volume 2.
You're working at your craft and ready to
move ahead. Being up in front of people
and playing a character, any character, is
good training. And an important part of it is
being **real**. True to the situation.
I can't tell you how many directors have
said to me "I don't want an '*actor-kid*'; I
want a real kid … who can act."

As we said in Volume 1: everybody acts.
Whether you ultimately become a
professional actor, or a teacher, salesman,
game designer or doctor … **everybody** acts.

Volume 2 is divided into four parts: acting
by yourself (monologues), acting in a scene
with someone near your age, acting with an
adult, and "shorty scenes" –quick scenes
with just a few lines each.

There are also "**Notes From The Coach**"
sprinkled throughout the book. These are
tips, questions or ideas about the characters
and the scenes for you to consider.

During each monologue or scene you'll play
a character that will experience a change,
learn a valuable lesson, be physical, imitate
someone else, or go for the comedy.

Most of the monologues and many of the scenes can be played by either a boy or a girl with just a minor adjustment or two. A few, such as "If I Only Had A Brain," are for a girl, and "Tree Streamers" is a boy prank.

For the **Monologues**, it's usually obvious who you're talking to; other times you have to pick someone, and it's important to put yourself in your character's shoes. How do they feel? What happened just before? What does your character want?

Same for the **Scenes,** and it's very important to LISTEN to what the other character is saying. And to listen *as your character listens:* **hearing it for the very first time.** Every time. And *take your time*; there are no prizes for finishing the fastest.

Re-acting is also essential. Play the "pauses". A great actor acts, reacts and interacts.

Another point -- last one, I promise -- there is a different dynamic when the scene is between a brother and sister, as opposed to a boy and a girl from school. Our tone is different when speaking to a sibling; that intimate familiarity can change our entire character and the way he or she speaks.

Ok. Let's do it. And have some fun.

MONOLOGUES

mon uh lawg - *noun*
a part of a drama, or comedic solo,
in which a single actor speaks alone;
soliloquy.

"Love the art in yourself, not yourself
in the art."

- *Konstantin Stanislavsky*

"Last Group Chat For A While"

Parker is at the computer. He/she is in pain, and in a video group-chat.

PARKER

Hey guys. I gotta go in a little bit, so … wish me luck. Some of you have been there, I know. Haley had her tonsils out; Charlie broke his arm. This is kind of like that, but kind of different too. They're going to cut right into my belly -- right here.
(points to his appendix)
Then they open me up, take out the appendix, and sew me back together again.   It really hurts now, but if I let it go, it might break. Burst, I mean, and then there's all kinds of trouble. So I won't see you all for a while. Maybe they'll let me have my tablet in a couple of days.
(sad smile)
Good thing my dad says it's okay to be scared. 'Cause I am. So … wish me luck. Wait, I already said that. Um, I gotta go. See you all later. Bye.

Parker closes the computer, looks at the door, grabs a backpack and bravely exits.

"Baby Secret"

DARBY

Hey, you wanna know a secret? Well,
if I tell you it won't be a secret
anymore … but I'll tell you.
I'm gonna have a baby sister. Real
soon. My mom's belly is way out to
here already.
(holds out hands)
And she went to the doctor and got
this little picture and you can see the
baby in it. All scrunched up like this:
(bends in fetal position)
I think she'll straighten out when she
comes out.
And I get to be the big sister.* I'm
gonna be a good big sister, and teach
her everything she needs to know.
Like how to wash between her toes in
the bathtub, to stay away from the
fireplace, and how much milk to put
on her cereal. Yeah. I'm gonna be a
good big sister.

* or brother

"We Got A Dog!"

McNALLY

We finally got a dog! Wait 'til you
see him. We went to the shelter
yesterday – there were SO many dogs,
it was so noisy – and the first cage we
saw had this poor little puppy sitting
on the cement looking at me. He had
such sad eyes, like this …
  (imitates: paws up, eyes big)
… so I bent down near him and said
"hi, little buddy" and **GROWWLL!**
He jumped at the cage and snapped at
my face! Sorry, no.
So we looked a little more and then---
I saw him. The cutest little half Lab,
half Pointer. As soon as I saw him I
knew, and he knew too. He stood on
his back legs and licked my fingers,
and yipped at me like he was saying
  (puppy voice)
*"C'mon, take me home. Let me be
your dog."*
And so I did. I named him Rocky.
He's my dog.

"If I Only Had A Brain"

SOPHIE

When I was little, at bedtime my dad would come in to my bedroom and sing something. Sometimes it was a goofy song, or one we heard in the car, or a Beatles song --- he loves the Beatles.
But most of the time it was the scarecrow's song "If I Only Had A Brain" from The Wizard of Oz. We did it enough that he would leave out words and let me sing them. Like he'd sing (his voice) "*I would not be just a nuthin', my head all full of* _____. And I'd sing "s*tuffin'*!"

But one day when he started to sing I told him I was too old for that now, and he could just say 'goodnight' to me. He didn't say anything for a while, then turned on the nightlight and said "Ok. Good night." And every night since, with a little smile he'd whisper 'goodnight' and leave.

I didn't say anything for a long time, but I missed it. I liked seeing him have fun singing to me. He once said it was his favorite minute of the day.

She pauses, regrets taking that minute away.

SOPHIE (cont'd)

So last night I asked if we could sing
again. And that little smile of his got
big. I picked the scarecrow's song
and we sang the whole thing together.
*"I could think of things I never
thought before. And then I'd sit ...
and think some more."*
I should never have told him I'm too
old for him.
If I only had a brain.

*This song is the Scarecrow's song from the
film "The Wizard of Oz". You can google
the melody.*

© Bo Kane

13

"Bully For Me"

LUCAS is standing in the hall at school.

LUCAS

This hallway is where the initiation
happens; a guy comes to this school,
he has to go through me. I own this
hall and you have to pay to go
through it.
    (pause)
Bullying is such a nasty word. I
prefer to think of it as a business deal.
You pay me, and your head stays on
your neck.
So yesterday this new kid comes
down the hall and tries to walk right
past me, like I was invisible. I told
him "Hey, you want to walk through
here it'll cost you $3." He says no
thanks.
What? Did you not hear me? He says
no again and tries to walk on.
That's not how it works. So I go to
push him and he side-steps me. That
is a no-no. Sorry, but I have to re-
arrange your face. I take a swing at
him, and next thing I know I'm on the
floor, and he has my arm behind my
back.
He whispers, "I said '*no*'" and walks
away.

LUCAS (cont'd)

And now the hall isn't empty
anymore---everybody saw this new
kid, who it turns out was a karate
champ from California, put me on the
floor.
I guess I have to find a new line of
work.
            (throws his backpack on)
Hard to make a buck these days.

                            He exits.

*"Courage is being scared to death,
        but saddling up anyway."*

                            - John Wayne

Notes from the Coach:

* In "Last Group Chat" (pg. 9) really see and talk to your friends in that computer. Feel the pain and the uncertainty.

* In "Baby Secret" (pg. 9) Darby shows (not just tells) the baby's size and position.

* In "We Got A Dog!" (pg. 11), really help us see the dog with your impersonations. Make that growl startle us, then show us the pride.

* You can use "If I Only Had A Brain", or sing your own song. But put yourself in dad's shoes, feel both his loss and his joy.

* Our "Bully" (pg. 14) has a good sense of humor, but … feel his humiliation when he gets beat.

* In "Cat Wishes" (pg. 17) you can physically get down by the cat, talk to it sideways in the middle, to make it more fun to play.

• Our "Tree Streamers" prankster (pg. 18) relives the tossing of the toilet paper with great pride. Let's see that enthusiasm, followed ultimately by the "uh-oh".

• "Box Top Benefits" (pg. 19) gives Sara the chance to show us her transformation in both expression and tone of voice. Let's see her go from "annoyed" to pleasantly surprised.

"What Do You Think?"

MORGAN

We had an extra 10 minutes in class
today, so our teacher told us to get out
some paper and write the answer to
this question: *What do you think?*
That's it. Usually it's 'what do you
want to be when you grow up?' or
'what person would you like to meet
and why?' but this was just 'What do
you think?' I asked what he meant by
that and he said "*What do you think?*"
I should have seen that coming.

So I wrote that I think we should have
less homework, and that all braces
should be on the inside of our teeth. I
think ghosts are real and rainbows are
beautiful. I think that wars are
stupid, and music is great. Singing a
song should be our homework.
And I think I'd like to be a doctor,
figuring out what's wrong with people
and then helping them.
I think that would make me happy.
Then the bell rang and we turned
them in. And I thought about this
assignment all the way home. Hmf.
Maybe that's what it was all about.

"Cat Wishes"

A not-too-happy ALEX comes in to the bedroom, drops her books, then looks at the cat lounging on her bed.

ALEX

Aren't you the lucky one? You don't have homework in spelling, and you don't have boys sitting in front of you making noises with their armpits do you? No, you just get to lie around all day, maybe eat a little bit, then go out in the yard and watch the butterflies. Maybe climb a tree if you want.   I wish I were a cat.
(gets near the cat)
And if I was the cat and you were me, I'd roll over and let <u>you</u> scratch <u>my</u> belly for a change.
And then you'd go get <u>my</u> food, and I'd be the one who hears the can opener and comes in meowing. How would that be? But…. I guess you can't tell me when you don't feel good. And when you cough up hairballs all over. So I guess … No, wait---you don't have to clean it up, we do. It's like you have maid service too. Yeah, I'd be a cat. What a life.

"Tree Streamers"

JUSTIN runs in to Michael's bedroom.

JUSTIN

Michael, wait 'til you hear this---first, promise not to tell Mom or Dad. Promise? Ok, did I tell you that Mia told on Jacob for having his phone out in class? She did; class was already over and she went up to the teacher and told on him, so the teacher finds Jacob in the hallway, takes away his phone AND gives him detention.

Well, tonight Jacob got me and a couple of other guys and we each brought a roll of toilet paper and guess where we went?! Mia's house. She's got two trees in front and we sent streamers up to the top of them. Shoom! You can't even see the house we tp'd it so well! It was epic! Hey, remember, whatever you do, don't tell mom because … what?
Oh…She's standing right behind me, isn't she?

"Box Top Benefits"

SARA discovers the benefits of charity.

SARA

Ok, two things happened Monday,
and one leads to the other. First, I
was eating cereal and watching a
video on my phone when my mother
asks where I put the boxtop. The
what? Apparently it has a coupon on
it so the school can buy textbooks and
… I don't know—trombones.
I had to go out to the recycle bin and
get it.
Anyway, second thing … so
I go to school trying to hide these
stupid cereal coupons; all I want to do
is give 'em to the lady and get out of
that office. And while I'm standing
there, in walks Wyatt, quite possibly
the cutest boy in the universe but
certainly the best in our grade. What
does he have in his hand? Coupons.
From cereal boxes! He sees mine and
says, "*Hey, Sara. You collect these
too huh? They really buy the school a
lot of stuff; cool of you to help.*" I
didn't even know he knew I was
alive. Then he smiled and said '*see
you around.*' Yes. Yes he will.

"Movin' Up, 1959"

1959, Midwest, USA. KATHY is packing up her clothing in the basement.

KATHY

I'm movin' upstairs now; gonna have a room like everybody else. My room. No more cold walls with daddy longlegs on 'em. I'm movin' to the bedroom that should have been mine in the first place. His "office." Yeah right. Never did anything but drink beer and watch Twilight Zone in there.

And now…he's gone. Finally. Never did treat my mama right. Complainin' all the time, slap her around if his meal wasn't exactly perfect. Last week after he yelled at her and stormed out I said, "Mama, I don't know why you stay married to him. He has never been nice to you not once in my whole life." That hit mama hard; she just looked at me kind of stunned. Half-crying, half-determined. Two days later the cops and the judge told him "you've got to go." And now I'm moving upstairs. Mama and I painted it 'lavender'. It's not an office anymore; it's my room.

© Bo Kane

"Act ... Like Spiderman"

Michael gets inspired by a movie on tv...

MICHAEL

I was watching this tv show last night
and it had this kid in it who solved all
these crimes before the police did, and
he had the gangsters chasing him all
over the city. And I thought 'this is
so cool; I bet I could do that.'
So I told my dad that I think I'd be a
good actor. He thought about it and
then said *"what kind of acting do you
want to do?"*

So I told him I'd like to do comedy,
but I also want to do action-adventure.
Maybe play a super-hero. He thought
about it again, and then asked me *"are
you willing to do the work?"*

I said, "What kind of work?" He told
me the action-adventure guys not only
have to work on their acting skills ---
learn all their lines, figure out the
character --- but they also have to
work out and be able to do stunts.

He said it was a lot like pro football
players, or professional guitar players;
it takes a lot of work and 'focus'.

MICHAEL (cont'd)

So I watched another show, and I thought "yeah. I would put the work in. Seems like you have to work hard no matter what you do, why not do something cool?"
So I'm going to; I'll be in the play at school, take an acting class, and I'm on the soccer team. Yeah. I'm going to be an actor. They'll still be doing Spiderman movies when I'm old enough to play him.

Michael ducks under an imaginary punch, then slings his "web" at the bad guy.

MICHAEL (cont'd)

This could be awesome.

Exit *(with style)*

NOTES FROM THE COACH

*   In "Movin' Up" (pg. 21) you'll notice the
    year is 1959. Times were different and so
    was the style of speech. Kathy has a
    resolve; she does not for a moment feel
    sorry for herself. You can give her a light
    accent if you like, but certainly give the
    performance the real, raw truth.

*   In "Spiderman" (page 22) Michael can give
    his dad a thoughtful, studied voice that is
    different from his own. Have fun at the
    end, but play it real with the punches.

*   "Play Outside" (25) is simply done with
    energy, one of the few where you play right
    to camera.

*   In "The Smokin' Truth" (28) there's no need
    to whine. Just state the facts, then come up
    with an 'almost the whole truth' solution.

*   In "Tom Sawyer" (29) Chad has to hear the
    aunt —listen and react. It's a fun scene, but
    take your time to hear the other end of the
    conversation.

*   "Mom's Promotion" (32) deals with a real
    dilemma and Kelly has that conflict in her
    voice and in her face. Talk to your (down-
    stage) brother; make him a real brother.

"Play Outside!"

QUINN is holding a microphone doing a news report for The Kids' Health Network.

QUINN

Hi. This is Quinn Smith reporting for 'The Kids' Health Network'.
Most doctors agree that we need sixty minutes of physical activity every day. A full hour. And they mean actual activity, not playing video games.
Playing outside helps build strong muscles and bones, keeps your body lean, and it's fun.
So if you want to live a long and happy life, you have to exercise more than just your thumbs. Get outside and play!
This is Quinn Smith reporting for The Kids' Health Network. Now back to you in the studio.

"The Nap Report"

KADEN is forced to rest....

KADEN

My mom made me take a nap again, and I wasn't even doing anything wrong. I yawned during a video--- just stretched and yawned---and the next thing you know the shutters are closed and I'm in bed. On a Saturday!

I'm __ years old and she treats me like I'm 4. My grandpa calls naps "mini vacations" but I don't. I call them jail.

The weird thing is---I have the strangest nap dreams. Not like at night. This one, I was back in kindergarten, but my cousins from Florida were there too, and my Aunt Jessica was the teacher.

She asked what we wanted to be when we grew up and I said "Superman". POOF! She took out this Harry Potter wand and I was flying through the air. And I saved this girl Sasha from a burning house. She's a girl from my 2nd grade class; I hadn't thought about her in over a year.

continued

26

KADEN (cont'd)

And after I saved her from the fire, a spaceship landed. And just as the aliens were getting out --- I woke up. Hmf. Why was I thinking about Sasha? And what did the aliens look like? It's like the book ended in the middle.

Next time I have to take a nap, I'll think of that spaceship landing and try to get back into that dream. Maybe, if I concentrate real hard, I can finish it. And then ... I'll turn it in for a book report! I'll get something out of these naps.

"The Smoking Truth"

Mom is getting ready to go to her sister's house. TAYLOR comes up with an excuse.

TAYLOR

Mom, can I **not** go to Aunt Sue and Uncle Don's house? Could you say I'm sick? No, wait, I don't want you to lie. Lying is bad.

How about … that you forgot I had a 'party' to go to? I'll go over to Tyler's or somebody's house and you can just say I wasn't home.

It's not that I don't like them; I do, but …it's just that they smoke all the time. Their whole house smells like smoke even when they're not smoking. I hate that smell.

So if I call Tyler and tell her to invite me over for a couple of hours, and you tell Aunt Sue and Uncle Don that I was at my friend's house for a 'party' --- don't worry, we'll have fun so you could *technically* call it a party --- then that's not lying. Is it?

She looks hopefully at mom, waits for the reaction.

"Tom Sawyer Lesson"

CHAD is vacuuming when he feels his phone vibrate in his pocket. He shuts off the vacuum and answers it.

CHAD

Hello? Oh, hey Aunt Viv ... no, Mom doesn't get home until tomorrow. It's just me and dad here, and he's letting me use the vacuum! ... Yeah. At first he said no, that it's a machine and I'm not ready to handle it yet. He was afraid I might bang in to the furniture or get something stuck in the motor, but I convinced him that I can handle it and be careful. ... Tom who? ... Tom Sawyer? No ... it's a book? Ok, Mark Twain, got it. I'll look it up. But AFTER I finish vacuuming.
Well, I gotta fire this beast up again. When Mom gets home I'll tell her you called. Bye. *(pockets the phone)*
Tom Sawyer can wait.
(looks at carpet)
Hey little fuzz-ball, YOU are history.

He fires it up and vacuums with a purpose.

"Driving Me Crazy"

HARPER

My dad is a pretty good driver, but his
brother …whew. We were driving to
Magic Coasters and my dad was in
the front with him, and me and my
cousin Mo were in the back. And
things were fine, for about 5 minutes.

Then when we were on the highway a
guy swerved in front of us and made
him slam on his brakes. And I
learned two more words I can't say
out loud. I mean, yeah, the driver was
rude, but he can't hear my uncle
screaming at him.
But we sure could…. *You rotten
blankey-blank, what the blank is
wrong with you—you're gonna kill
somebody!"* If there really was a chill
pill, I would've given it to him.

Then my cousin Mo reached into a
backpack and pulled out two big sets
of headphones and handed me one. I
was kind of surprised she had two
sets, but she just nodded for me to put
them on.
We plugged in to her phone and
listened to music the rest of the way.

HARPER (cont'd)

Then we had a great time at the park … we rode four coasters and a two splash rides.   One of the coasters was really scary—I mean, <u>really</u> scary. Almost as scary as the ride home with my uncle.

"Try not to know something before your character knows it; play the moment your character is in. If he doesn't know that after he crosses the street his ice cream is going to fall off the cone and into the dog's mouth, then try to play him not knowing it until then. Let him be happy as he crosses the street."

© Bo Kane

"Mom's Promotion"

KELLY is awake, looks at her brother.

KELLY

Scotty, you still awake? I can't sleep either. (sigh) It's tomorrow. They're coming *tomorrow*. I know we're supposed to be thinking about Mom, how happy she is to get this promotion. It is a big deal. Even Dad is quitting his job for her, but ... I don't want to leave. I don't want to make new friends; I don't want new teachers. I want the friends I already have.
But the movers are coming tomorrow. And Dad says "no whining" when Mom is around. So this is it; last time you'll hear me complaining. Mom does so much for us, so ... smiling face for Mom. And, at least we have each other, right? Right?

She looks at his happy sleeping face.

KELLY (cont'd)
G'night Scotty. You're right: just go to sleep. Tomorrow's gonna happen, whether I'm ready or not.
(she closes her eyes)
Just be brave.

NOTES FROM THE COACH:

* There are a few layers for Carly to play in "Jenna's Dilemma" (pg 34). She is animated and big when she talks about Jenna's dad's truck and mom's feeling toward his girlfriend, but she is also small and sympathetic when she describes Jenna's exit in the truck (show us). And her solution, and her gratitude to her parents, is sincere.

* In "My Friend's Back!" (page 36), apart from the obvious energy, there is an "aside". Something Erin says, *"not complaining, everybody did"* apart from her enthusiastic sentence… in a different tone. Maybe a flatter tone. Experiment.

* "Ring Pop" (page 37) is just a fun bit where Jay really works dad over. You've done it yourself, haven't you?

* In "Tossin Trash" (pg 40) the PSA part is played right to camera. Lots of interaction on this one. The 'aside' is the meatless revelation.

* "Poetry" (pg 42) needs little explanation. I think it's funnier not to say the word in Andrew's 'poem' but to **almost** say it. Good timing on the interruptions.

"Jenna's Dilemma"

CARLY unpacks her backpack and explains to Mom why her friend Jenna isn't with her.

CARLY

Okay, so Jenna was supposed to walk home with me today and hang out here, but then she got a text saying that her dad was going to pick her up instead. They're having <u>his</u> weekend start early because, as you know, Jenna is coming with us on Sunday.

Well, Jenna's mom said he could have her today, instead of Sunday. That was their "arrangement".
Her mom and dad don't really like each other; they don't even pretend anymore. And her mom REALLY doesn't like the lady that lives with Jenna's dad.
> *(puts her claws up and snarls like a cat)*

Her dad is that exterminator, you know? He drives a big truck that says "KILLS BUGS DEAD!", and has that 3-D man hitting a cockroach on the head with a hammer on top of it.
I think it's funny; Jenna hates it.
> *(more)*

34

CARLY (cont'd)
So after school she got into the bug
truck, and when they drove away she
looked out the window like this …
(sad face, small wave)
I'm glad you and dad are still
together. Really glad.
Hey, when Jenna comes over on
Sunday, do you think we could go see
a movie? A funny one? I think she
could use a comedy.

*The pages of a script that we are reading for an
audition are called 'sides'.*

"My Friend's Back!"

ERIN excitedly rushes in to the kitchen …

ERIN

You'll never guess who I saw at the pool! Brody Johnson! She's back! Remember? We were best friends in kindergarten and first grade, then she moved away – to somewhere in Michigan.

I was walking over to the diving board and there she was. We didn't recognize each other at first, then it was "Ahhhkkk!!! We got so excited. She had tried to call but we got rid of our landline -- not complaining, everybody did—and she hadn't enrolled yet, and … oh, who cares?! She's back! This is going to be the best summer ever!

(Erin exits, then turns back)
By the way, she's coming over in ten minutes. We should clean up a little bit.

"Ring Pop"

JAY shows his ring pop to his friend.

JAY

My dad had to work from home
today, and my mom is on night shift
at the hospital, so Dad had to go to the
grocery store. Which meant I had to
go too. (*dad voice*) "If I'm going,
you're going." Not a big thrill for me.
Once you leave the cereal and cookie
aisle, it's pretty boring. 'What's your
toothpaste? What kind of vegetables
do you want?' Seriously? None.
I couldn't even get any real speed
going on the back of the shopping cart
because it was so crowded.
We finally got to the checkout and I
see this red-sour Ring Pop. I said
"Dad, will you get this ring pop for
me?" And he says 'Two dollars!?
No, put it back.'
So **I** said, "Let me ask this another
way … if I promise NOT to tell Mom
that YOU'RE the one who spilled a
milkshake in her new car and made it
stink inside … will you buy me this
ring pop?"
He calls it blackmail. I call it
'effective negotiation.'

"When actors are talking, they are the servants of the dramatist. It is what they can show the audience when they are not talking that reveals the fine actor."

- Cedric Hardwicke

Acting Scenes

Scene [seen] - *noun*
a unit of action or a **segment of a
story** in a play, motion picture, or
television show.

"Tossin' Trash"

LUCY and PAIGE rehearse their presentation in front of Paige's big sister.

PAIGE
We have to do a media presentation, so we picked a Public Service Announcement.

LUCY
It's a PSA about cleaning up the beaches ... see what you think.

PAIGE
Ahem...(to camera) Hi, I'm Paige.

LUCY
And I'm Lucy. We both like a lot of the same things: we both like movies.

PAIGE
Especially comedies.

LUCY
Romantic comedies for me. And we like hip hop music.

PAIGE
And cheeseburgers!

LUCY *(to Paige)*
Actually, I don't eat red meat.

PAIGE
Oh. Did not know that. Scratch the
burger ad-lib.

LUCY *(to camera)*
And we both like summers at the
beach.

PAIGE
But there's one thing we don't like —
littering.

JAMIE
Littering can turn a paradise … into a
dump.

Jamie picks up a can and a candy wrapper.

PAIGE
So enjoy your food and drink, and
then find a trash can.

JAMIE
Let's keep our parks and beaches
clean.

PAIGE (or BOTH)
'Cause tossin' trash … ain't cool.

41

"Poetry: Good For The Heart"

MAE is looking through a poetry book when ANDREW walks in.

ANDREW
What'cha doing?

MAE
I have to find a poem to read in class. Do you know any poems?

ANDREW
Sure. Beans beans, they're good for your heart, the more you eat, the…

MAE
Not that kind!! I need one that will move people, inspire them.

ANDREW
Inspire them to do what?

MAE
I'm not sure. Wait, here's one"

"I wish I could take those words back. Could put them back in my mouth. I was trying to be funny, but it came out mean. And suddenly things went south.
(more)

MAE (cont'd)
*"Once the genie is out of the
bottle it's hard for him to come
back. So from now on I'll
watch my words. And
cut my friends some slack."*

ANDREW
That's pretty good; words can hurt,
and ... whatever else you said.
But hey, there's also a second one of
mine: "Beans, beans the musical
fruit. The more you eat, the...

MAE
Stop it! Enough about beans!   Here,
Stinky, read some real poetry.

She throws the book at him and exits.

ANDREW
The more you eat, the more you
toot. Heheh.

43

"Unfriended"

ELIZABETH and KARI are sitting in a McDonald's.

BETH

I haven't seen Vanessa in a while, have you?

KARI

No, we're not friends anymore.

BETH

Why? What happened?

KARI

I don't know. Some of us went to the concert at the mall and we didn't invite her and she flipped out on me. So I unfriended her.

BETH

Oh. When was that?

KARI

Last week; what difference does it make? She got all weird; I don't need that…
(looks at Beth's knowing face)
What?

BETH

Vanessa's brother left about a week
ago. Her mom moved her grand-
mother in, and, I don't know, I guess
her brother couldn't take it, so he left.
And you know how she idolizes her
big brother.

KARI

Oh no. I didn't even ask her about…
Her life was crazy and I told her to
'just chill'. This is terrible.

BETH

You didn't know.

KARI

Because I didn't ask. I'm a horrible
person.

She buries her head in her hands.

BETH

Well, you did kick when she was
down. There's that "walk a mile
in my shoes" thing. I mean, when
somebody flips out for no reason,
instead of getting mad, you might be
curious about, you know …

Kari lifts her head, stares at Beth.

KARI

Are you done?

BETH

Yep.

KARI

Ok. I have to fix this. I will friend
her again and say I'm sorry. And then
I'll go see her.

She pulls out her phone and types.

BETH

You know, you didn't invite me to the
concert at the mall either.

KARI

Sorry. Here, have some of my fries.
We good?

BETH

We're cool.

She eats the fries as Kari tries to make
amends.

"Charity Begins At Home"

CHRIS is stuffing clothing into a sack when WILL enters his house.

> WILL
> Hey, Chris, you want to go over to the skate park?

> CHRIS
> Yeah, soon as I finish putting these shirts and stuff in the giveaway bag.

> WILL
> (looks at the clothes)
> This stuff?

> CHRIS
> Yeah. I don't really wear these anymore. And those don't fit me, so we're giving them to charity.
> They'll fit somebody.

> WILL
> (holding up a shirt)
> Bro, I don't know anybody who can't afford a shirt. Especially a used one.

> CHRIS
> Seriously? Okay, well, your parents
> *(more)*

CHRIS (cont'd)
both went to college, and my dad
became an engineer in the Navy; but
some kids don't have that. Some
don't even have a dad.

WILL
Hmf. Whose fault is that?

Chris exhales, tries to explain....

CHRIS
Last time I was there a little boy
walked in with his mom. He was
maybe six, skinny kid with big eyes,
and he was so happy to get the
clothes they gave him. And he got an
old baseball glove, and his mom got
some soup and rice and ... you could
see they really needed it.
So I don't know whose fault it was,
but I know this---it wasn't that little
boy's fault.

He throws the now-full bag over his
shoulder.

CHRIS (cont'd)
Come on. I'll leave this for my mom
and we'll go skate.

WILL
Hey, wait. Ya know, I've got some
old stuff I don't wear anymore.
When's your mom going?

On Chris' surprised look, Will shrugs a *'ok,
you convinced me'*.

CHRIS
Tomorrow. Let's go get your stuff.

They exit.

Curses! Cursive!"

MO is writing/crossing out words and getting frustrated when HARLEY comes up.

MO
Arrgghh!! This is so dumb.

HARLEY
What are you doing?

MO
Cursive. I print the line, then I have to "write" it.

HARLEY
Our teacher doesn't use cursive.

MO
Mrs. Lane showed us the Declaration of Independence and it has all these names written at the bottom.   Then she asked how many of us knew how to write our name. Zero. No one in our class knew how to sign their name. So now we're learning cursive.

HARLEY
Well, when you get old you have to sign your name all the time. My dad's a lawyer and he has people sign their name every day.

MO
Can you sign your name?

HARLEY
Yeah. My signature is the only thing
I can write, but yeah.

MO
A signature … my own signature.
Like that Hancock guy. Ok, maybe
this won't be so bad.

Mo goes back to 'writing'. Harley leans
over and looks at the paper.

HARLEY
Um, I think that loop goes on the
other side.

MO
Arrgghh!!

Mo crosses it out again.

"Splash Attack"

At the swimming pool, ELI is sitting on the penalty bench when CADE comes up.

CADE
I've been looking for you, Eli. What did you do?

ELI
Aw, I snuck up on Bella and splashed her in the face and her friend went whining to the Lifeguard.

Cade drops his smile immediately.

CADE
Whoa. You're the one…

ELI
One what? I was just …

CADE
(interrupting)
She's over by the concession stand with an ice pack on her eye. You didn't just splash her, you whacked her eye.

ELI
I was only … it was an accident. I didn't mean to hurt her.

CADE

Well, you did. And all her friends are mad at you too. You gotta go apologize.

ELI

I can't. They won't let me leave this bench for 15 more minutes.

CADE

No good. You gotta go now and tell her you're sorry. Hey – I'll put this towel over my head and sit here; the lifeguard will think it's you. Go.

ELI

You're right. Thanks. I'll be right back.

They switch places.

CADE

Don't make it worse.

Eli begins his march to humiliation.

"Splash Attack 2"

BELLA holds her hand over her injured eye. ANGIE holds an ice cream cone in one hand, peeks through Bella's fingers with the other.

> ANGIE
>
> It doesn't look too bad. I think the cold pack helped. I can't believe he hit you like that

> BELLA
>
> He didn't mean to hit me; I think he just meant to splash me and he got too close.

> ANGIE
>
> Boys are so stupid sometimes. Most of the time.

> ELI (O.S.)
>
> Yeah. We are.

They turn, surprised to see him.

> ELI
>
> I'm sorry, Bella.

> ANGIE
>
> You should be, you almost poked her eye out!

Bella gives her a tap to 'cool it'.

> BELLA
> It'll be alright.

> ELI
> I didn't mean to touch you, I just …
> I wish I could make it up to you.

Bella looks forgiving. Eli glances away, sees Angie's ice cream.

> ELI (cont'd)
> Angie, I'll give you the money for this is a minute.

Eli scoops the ice cream out of Angie's cone, puts it in Bella's hand. He leans his face forward.

> ELI
> Go ahead, hit me with it.

> BELLA
> No, I'm not going to hit you.

> ANGIE
> I'll hit him!

ELI

Go ahead. It'll make you feel better.
Really.

Bella thinks about it, looks like she won't do
it, then winds up and SMASHES the ice
cream right in Eli's face. Every kid laughs,
even Angie. Eli doesn't try to clean it off;
takes his punishment with a half smile.

BELLA

You're right. I do feel better.

ELI

Told ya. I really am sorry.
*(wipes his eye, it stings. Looks
at Angie)*
Salted Caramel? Really?

ANGIE

Aww, does it sting?

They all laugh. He gets a towel, waves
good-bye.

NOTE: *You can ball up the middle of a
slice of bread to use as the ice cream.*

© Bo Kane

56

NOTES FROM THE COACH

* In "Charity Begins At Home" (pg 47) Will has a breakthrough. Chris is not condescending, but explains it the way it was explained to him by his (very good) parents.

* You've seen the Declaration of Independence and you know what Mo envisions in "Curses! Cursive!" (50) If not, take a look at the flair on those signatures.

* "Splash Attack 1 and 2" deal with Eli's mistake, and how to correct it. He runs through denial, confusion, and then owning up. Angie is a fireball; have fun with her.

* "Dancin' Fool" (pg. 58) only requires just a few easy dance steps. You can use the one in the scene (google 'dance grapevine' for the video) or make up your own.

* In "Funeral Party" (60) Morgan not only tells the story of her late grandfather, but *shows* us how he had fun (kicking the ball, sneaking the ice cream). From the heart.

* "Special Kid" (62) requires some care to make Riley a character, not a caricature. He feels the pressure, but doesn't lose his sense of humor. And he really appreciates Sam; she (or he) is the friend we all want.

* At one point in "...Zoo" (pg 64) Katie interrupts Cody. Cody won't just stop, he'll add a 'you know' or stammer until she breaks in. Timing.

"Dancin' Fool"

TREVOR sees Marley in the hallway.

TREVOR
Marley! Just the girl I was looking for.

MARLEY
Ooh, I don't like the sound of that. What do you want, Trevor?

TREVOR
I'm trying out for the musical, and I need some help.

MARLEY
Oh. That's not as bad as I thought it would be. What do you need?

TREVOR
I have a monologue, but I also need to show them some dancing --- which I've never done. But you're a good dancer; could you show me a few easy steps? Emphasis on "easy".

MARLEY
Just a few steps? Sure. How about a grapevine?

He looks at her like she just spoke Swahili.

MARLEY (cont'd)
Here, stand next to me and follow.
We'll go left and then come back.
Side step, behind, side and tap. So,
side, behind, side and tap.
And then we go back.

She does it with him a couple of times, back
and forth. Trevor slowly untangles his feet
and gets it. She tells him *"that's it, no in
front, behind; good, you're getting it! Keep
your head up."* He can even put a small dip
into it. Finally …

TREVOR
This is great, Marley, thanks a lot.

MARLEY
You're welcome. Break a leg.

Marley walks on.

TREVOR
Hey Marley! What did you think I
wanted when I first walked up?

MARLEY
Never mind.

He watches her go. Hmmm …

59

"Funeral Party"

QUINN sees MORGAN at the mall.

QUINN
Morgan! Didn't see you at band this
weekend. Where were you?

MORGAN
At my grandpa's funeral.

QUINN
Oh. Sorry. I didn't know. Must've
been really sad, huh?

MORGAN
I thought it would be, and my mom
was really sad on the way there. But
when we got there it was more like a
party than a funeral. Everyone was
telling stories about my grandpa and
laughing and joking.

QUINN
Really? Even at the funeral?

MORGAN
Yeah. My grandpa was a good guy.
The priest talked about how when
they played golf together my grandpa
would always 'kick' his ball out of
(more)

MORGAN

the sand trap. And when the priest
would catch him and say "ahem!"
Grandpa would look at his ball all
surprised and yell, "It's a miracle!"
They all laughed at that one.

QUINN

I've never been to a funeral like that.
Most of the time everyone is crying.

MORGAN

My grandpa didn't want that. He
used to take me to the park and to
Dairy Queen. But if you looked the
other way, he would bite off the top of
your ice cream and then look innocent
like this:
 (rolls eyes away and whistles)
And then he'd laugh and buy me
another one.

QUINN

He sounds like a fun grandpa.

MORGAN

He was…I'm gonna miss him.

"Special Kid"

RILEY, a former special ed student (now in regular class) looks miserable as OLIVIA approaches.

OLIVIA
Hey Riley, how are you doing? You ok?

RILEY
No. We just had a test in math. I didn't do too well. Some kids saw my grade. uuggghh!

OLIVIA
It's ok, don't get mad at yourself. We all get a lousy grade once in a while.

RILEY
I didn't like it when they made fun of me. 'Specially Drake. He's mean.

OLIVIA
I know. I'm sorry you got a bad grade, but you knew it would be tougher this year, right? And you're doing really well in regular school; it took a lot of guts to be here with all of those Drakes and …probably Marco too, right?

RILEY

Marco was even worse. He kept
calling me 'special' and 'tardo'. I
wish I could beat him up.

OLIVIA

Not that he doesn't deserve it, but
you're better than that. Try not to pay
attention to them, and next time you
have a hard test coming up, ask the
teacher for some help. And if that
doesn't work, I'll help you.

RILEY
(small smile)
Would you beat up Marco for me too?

OLIVIA

No problem. I'll tear him apart for
ya. (*smiles*) Nah, he'd kick my butt.
Let him be a jerk, we'll just work a
little harder. I gotta go. Text me if
you need help. Bye.

RILEY

Thanks. You're the best.

OLIVIA

Glad you noticed.

© Bo Kane

63

"It's All Happening At The Zoo"

CODY and KATIE are leaving school.

> KATIE
> Woo-hoo! We have tomorrow off.
> What are you going to do?

> CODY
> Same thing I always do---play video
> games.

> KATIE
> What kind of video games?

> CODY
> Assassin's Mission, where you shoot
> people, and Danger-zone, where you ..

> KATIE
> *(interrupts)*
> Shoot people, got it. We're going to
> the zoo tomorrow. Zeke is coming
> and my cousin. Wanna go?

> CODY
> The zoo? What's at the zoo?

> KATIE
> Seriously?

CODY

I mean, what's *interesting* at the zoo?

KATIE

Last time we were there the elephants
were swimming by us with these huge
toys, and we made faces on the glass
and I swear they were laughing at us.
And the chimps are always funny.

CODY

I don't know …

KATIE

And the giraffes had a baby; I want to
see how big it is now. Their tongues
are purple and super long. Well, have
fun shooting people. See you later.

CODY

Ok. … uh, wait. I'll probably finish
conquering the Templars tonight. I
could go with you, if you want.

KATIE

Sure! Pick you up at 9. Bring a
couple of dollars for giraffe food; they
eat right out of your hand.

She raises her eyebrows, smiles, and exits.

"Frame The Star"

McKENNA sees KADEN at lunch....

McKENNA
Hey Kaden, I'm making a Youtube
video! Want to be in it?

KADEN
What's it about?

McKENNA
I don't know yet. But it has to be
funny or it won't get lots of views.
Maybe a funny prank. Can you act?

KADEN
Not really.

McKENNA
Sing? Dance?

AIDAN
Not even close. Thanks anyway.
Good luck.

McKENNA
Wait! You can hit and catch a
baseball; that means you have good
eyes. And you're strong...you're my
cameraman!

KADEN

What? McKenna, the only camera
I've ever used is my phone.

McKENNA

Don't worry. I'll put it on auto-focus.
Just frame the shot and make me look
good. Kidding – I'll handle that part.
Ok, I'm the actress, so all I need is a
story, a script, some extras, and props.
Easy peasy. It'll be great!

She starts to go, then turns back.

McKENNA (cont'd)

By the way, we start shooting
tomorrow!

KADEN

Tomorrow!?!
(she's gone)
O-kay. I'm a cameraman. It'll be
funny alright.

He gets up, frames an imaginary shot with
his fingers, then thinks back...

KADEN (cont'd)

She called me 'strong'.

"Rumor Has It"

KELLY walks up to the hallway locker,
feels the stares from the other kids. He (she)
is met by ANDY.

> KELLY
>
> What's going on?

> ANDY
>
> Everybody's talking about you. Are
> you ok?

> KELLY
>
> Yeah. Why?

Kelly looks again at the curious kids.

> ANDY
>
> We heard about the fight. And we
> thought you might be injured.

> KELLY
>
> Injured? What fight?

> ANDY
>
> The fight! Your fight! Oh, ok, sorry,
> you don't want to talk about it.

> KELLY
>
> I can't talk about it because I don't
> know what you're talking about.

ANDY

You and your brother! The other
night. Maxy walked by your house
and heard everything. Did your
brother … did he go to jail?

KELLY

No, he went to the theater.

ANDY

They jailed him in a theater?!

KELLY

No. He got a part in a play at the
Starlight; he's playing a tough juvey
kid who gets in a fight. I was just
helping him rehearse. I guess next
time we better close the windows.

ANDY

Whoa. And that rumor spread fast!
EVERYBODY thinks you were in a
fight. I guess we better tell them …

KELLY

No wait; hold on. I was in a fight...
and came out without a scratch.
Let's let it go. This could be good.

Devious smiles as they walk off.

© Bo Kane

"Cereal Prankster"

The OLDER SISTER sits at breakfast with her YOUNGER BROTHER.

BROTHER
Hey, why do you get the cereal with the berries in it, and I only get the plain flakes? ... I wanted pancakes.

SISTER
Mom doesn't have time to make you pancakes, she's going to work. And there's only one bowl of berry cereal left and it's mine.

BROTHER
Awwww.

SISTER
And no whining. When mom's gone I'm in charge: you do what I tell you to do, eat what I tell you to eat and tell me everything that's going on, good or bad. You report to me, got it?

BROTHER
I guess so. Well, here's my report: there's a lotta bugs in your closet.

SISTER
What!?!

BROTHER

I guess you dropped a chip on the floor. There's lots of bugs. Way in the back too.

The Big sister jumps up

SISTER

I hate bugs ... uhhh, my new shoes!

She RUNS out. He slides her bowl of cereal over to his side. Takes a bite.

BROTHER

That was too easy.

Eats with a smile.

"Halloween"

COOPER is at the kitchen table looking at pictures of costumes when GIGI enters.

COOPER
What are you going to be for Halloween?

GIGI
Halloween is two months away.

COOPER
Right! Can't wait. So what's gonna be your costume?

Gigi grabs some grapes and sits with him.

GIGI
I don't know. I just know I'm not going to be 'sweet'---no Tinkerbelles. This year I want to scare people.

COOPER
When I said I want to be scary Dad said '*go as the evening news*.' Not sure what that means. Hey, I can be a vulture with nasty wings, and hang a dead squirrel from my claws!

GIGI
Ycch! That's gross, not scary.

COOPER

Not a real squirrel. A fake one.
Ooh, how about this?---a SWAT guy!
I could get a water gun, storm up to
the porch and yell *"Trick or Treat!*
Now! Move! Move! Fire in the
hole!"

GIGI

You'll get a lot of doors slammed in
your face. I saw this shop that had
zombie masks; I could get one and put
fake blood over my eye ... with my
severed tongue hanging ...

COOPER
(interrupts)
Mom will NEVER let you do that.

GIGI

She won't let you be a squirrel-
killing vulture either. *(sigh)* I guess
we'll end up being Han Solo and
Princess Leia again.

COOPER

I hope not. *(pause)* But if we do, this
year I'M Han Solo!

He follows her out.

73

"What Do You Want To Be?"

TRE and DAKOTA are sitting on a ledge outside of school, waiting for their parents to pick them up.

DAKOTA
Our teacher is making us write 'what we want to be' when we grow up.

TRE
Mr. Davis gave us the same assignment. When I was in kindergarten I wrote that I wanted to be a fireman or a motorcycle cop because they got to drive really fast. But now I think it should be more important.

DAKOTA
Those are pretty important, and exciting. I was going to write that I'd be a lawyer like my dad. But that's not too exciting. Maybe I should say that I'm going to be a spy.
(foreign accent)
"I will uncover your secrets. One way ... or another."

TRE
That sounds good; being a spy would be cool. Now, for me ...what would be important and exciting?
(more)

74

TRE (cont'd)
What about an astronaut? I could go
to Mars in a spaceship!

DAKOTA
I saw astronaut training in science. I
think you'd throw up in that 'vomit
comet' that they spin you around in.
Being a policeman is important and
exciting.   But it's dangerous.
(sees Mom arrive)
Gotta go.
(starts to leave, then …
foreign accent)
"Good bye, and, good luck".

She's gone.

TRE
(to himself)
Hmm. Yeah. She's right. I'd
probably throw up. Motorcycle cop
it is.

He sees his mother drive up and runs out.

"Change of Climate"

Younger BROTHER is working on a poster board science project when his SISTER approaches.

> SISTER
> Is that your science project?

> BROTHER
> Yeah. I'm almost done. It's about climate change.

> SISTER
> You put the sun in the wrong spot. Put it over here.

She picks up the sun and re-tapes it to a different spot on the board.

> BROTHER
> What are you doing? <u>That's</u> where it goes!

> SISTER
> No, it doesn't, and your glacier is too big on top. It's supposed to be small, and the bottom could be bigger...

> BROTHER
> Just leave it alone. The sun goes back over here and the glacier is fine.

SISTER
Go ahead, put it there. I'm right and you're wrong, but go ahead. Get a "C" if you want to. F-Y-I, I never got a "C" in anything. Ever.

BROTHER
That's because teachers don't grade on mean-ness. They don't care if you're nice or not. If you're a "*I'm smarter than you*" pain in the neck.
(picks up his stuff)
They don't care, but the rest of us do.

He leaves.

SISTER
I'm still right!

He's gone; she's alone. She thinks about it: Am I too bossy? Do I only want to be right? Hmmm. (Does she take it to heart, or not care at all?)

NOTE: For the 'moveable' sun, try a post-it note.

"I Bet You're Right"

EMILY leans against her locker, unable to move, when MICHAEL sees her.

MICHAEL

Hey, Em. You okay?

EMILY

No. I just saw this accident and it kind of freaked me out. 'Cause I saw it in my head and then it happened.

MICHAEL

You saw it? Was it a bad accident?

EMILY

No, just a "bang!-crunch!" at the traffic light. Right in front of me.

MICHAEL

Were you in the street?

EMILY

No, I was riding in the car next to the lady who was texting and drinking coffee -- as she was driving! For like a mile. I said out loud: "I bet she gets into an accident." And a half mile later she hit this car that was stopped at the light. It's like I caused it.

MICHAEL
She wasn't paying attention. You
didn't say you HOPED she'd hit
someone or you WISHED she'd get
into an accident.

EMILY
I said 'I bet'.

MICHAEL
Doesn't count. Unless you used your
super telekinetic power to MAKE it
happen, it was her stupid texting and
driving that caused it. Not you. I
BET she doesn't do that again.

EMILY
You're right; it had nothing to do with
me. I don't know why I feel guilty.

Michael picks up a pencil like a wand…

MICHAEL
My wizardry will enter your brain.
Lose the guilt! Feel good again!
Voila'!

EMILY
Thank you.

MICHAEL
Magic at a discount. 5 bucks please.

NOTES FROM THE COACH

*   In "Frame The Star" (66) Kaden can't /
doesn't say 'no' but does he really want to?
His re-actions are very important. And, as
self-absorbed as McKenna is, she has
energetic charm.

*   "Rumor Has It" (68) has a touch of French
farce. Something was heard out of context
and taken to an extreme. Andy is that
excitable sidekick. We should see the idea,
the realization on Kelly's face at the end.

*   Let's try to make sure our "Cereal
Prankster" (pg 70) doesn't give away his
new plan too soon. Be very sincere about
the bugs (that don't exist).

*   In "Change of Climate" (pg 76) it may be
the 100th time that his sister has been bossy
and 'know-it-all' and he's had it. Feel like
you can show the passion. How does the
sister feel at the end? Show us.

*   Emily has a big emotional arc in "I Bet
You're Right" (pg 78). A bit in shock to
frustrated guilt to feeling blameless and
good. Michael is a good friend, and has fun
with his 'magical' flair (which could also be
like a televangelist with his hand on her
head shouting "heal!")

Acting Scenes with Adults

"Cat Tale"

An upset Austin runs in with a bleeding
scratch on his arm.

> AUSTIN
> Mom! Look at this—that stupid cat
> scratched me!

> MOM
> Oh, dear. What cat?

> AUSTIN
> That big one! You know … that one
> from down the block.

> MOM
> What were you doing to it?

> AUSTIN
> Nothing!

> MOM
> Did you step on its tail, or hit it …?

> AUSTIN
> No, I wasn't doing anything. It just
> reached out and bit me.

> MOM
> Wait. A moment ago you said it
> scratched you.

He stands frozen as she arches her eyebrow.

> MOM (cont'd)
> I'm going to go get some band-aids,
> and you're going to get your story
> straight.

She comes back to an embarrassed Austin.

> MOM (cont'd)
> Austin, what happened to your arm?

> AUSTIN
> Jesse and me found some big sticks
> and were sword-fighting.
> *(He holds out his arm)*
> I'm sorry.

> MOM
> I trust you to tell me the truth.
> Always.

> AUSTIN
> I will. Sorry mom.

> MOM
> Next time use pool noodles.

From embarrassed to *'that's a great idea.'*

"Poor Side Of Town"

ELLE gets in the car seat, slumps, frowning.

ELLE
Aarrgghh! Ok, I'm done now. Can we go?

MOM
Should I even ask?

ELLE
Lindsey told everyone she's going to the New York Dance Academy this summer.   **I** wanted to do that.

MOM
And I told you, we can't afford that one. It's incredibly expensive.

ELLE
I'm a better dancer than she is. I'll pay you back.

MOM
We don't have the tuition, period. Besides, Webster college has a great day camp right here.

ELLE
Thrilling.

MOM

Stop it. You know I'd like to send
you to New York. I can't. I'm sorry.
'It's not about having what you want,
it's about wanting what you've got.'
Sheryl Crow.

ELLE

I'm supposed to be happy we're poor?

MOM

You're supposed to be happy, period.
We have enough to send you to the
camp here, but not enough to send
you to New York. Sorry.

ELLE

Can't you borrow it?

She sees the answer is 'no'. Sighs and looks
out the car window. After a pause ...

MOM

Would a smoothie help?

ELLE

You sure we can afford it?

Mom is hurt by that. Her eyes get wet and
she stares straight ahead as she drives on.

85

ELLE (cont'd)
Hey, I'm sorry. Mom, the Juice It Up
is back that way.
(pause)
Mom, I didn't mean it. I shouldn't
have said that. Mom?

Mom wipes her eye.

MOM
Ok. You want a smoothie?

ELLE
No. I just want to take back what I
said. I'm really sorry.

END

"Note From Teacher"

AARON (ERIN) carries an envelope into the kitchen. Looks at Dad.

                    ERIN
         They want you to read this note and
         sign it. It's from my teacher.

                    DAD
         Ok. Is it a good note, or a bad one?

                    ERIN
         I don't know.

                    DAD
              (eyebrows arched)
         Ahem.

                    ERIN
         It's a bad one.

Erin (Aaron) sheepishly hands over the note.
Then …

                    ERIN (cont'd)
         But in my defense … all the kids
         thought it was funny!

"Daddy Rule Book – Football"

RUBEN sees his dad come through the door.

RUBEN
Hey Dad! You have to play football with me.

DAD
I do?

RUBEN
Yeah. It's in the Daddy Rule Book. It says that if you play with me, and I grow up to be a famous football player, you can watch me on tv.

DAD
It says all that, huh?

RUBEN
And because you played with me, when I grow up and make millions of dollars playing football, I'll give you some.

DAD
Tell you what: Daddy Rule Book says 'no charge'. Let's go!

Ruben smiles, tosses him the football, catches it and runs outside.

"Daddy Rule Book – Two For Tea "

SOPHIE has her tea party set, and sees Dad.

SOPHIE
Daddy! You have to play tea party
with me.

DAD
Is that right?

SOPHIE
Yep. It's in the Daddy Rule Book.
You get to sit right there and I'll pour
you some tea.

DAD
Ok. What kind of tea are we having?

SOPHIE
It's invisible tea. I made it myself.

She pours, and they clink cups and drink.

DAD
Cheers. Ahh. That's the best
invisible tea I've ever had.

EMMY
Thank you Daddy. You can go do
your work now if you want.

"Racing With The Wind"

COLBY is confident, stretching/warming up for a big race …when he hears his mother.

COLBY
Mo-om, they don't want parents near the track.

MOM
You forgot your inhaler. Here…

COLBY
Mom, don't. I didn't forget. I don't need it.

Colby pushes it back to her so no one sees it.

MOM
It will help you run better, believe me. Just a couple of inhales.

COLBY
Fine. Could you stand there so nobody sees me?
(inhales twice)

MOM
Very good. Ok, I'll be in the stands by the other parents. You'll hear me.

COLBY
Oh, I'm sure. *(he runs off)*.

NOTES FROM THE COACH

*   In "Cat Tale" (82) Austin really sells
his story ... mad and animated, until ...
he slips up. He then is truly sorry, a
complete change of emotion. Mom gives
him not only a pass, but a good idea.
Austin's face should show that appreciation.

*   We've all complained and made
someone feel badly for something out
of their control, and in "Poor Side Of
Town" (pg 84) Elle does just that.
Emotional scene.

*   At the end of "Two For Tea" (pg 89)
there is an opportunity to eliminate
Sophie's last line, and let dad and Sophie
ad-lib. Dad could ask why she was upset
earlier, what he should get Mommy for their
anniversary, where should they go on
vacation, etc. Good chance to improv.

*   In "Racing With The Wind" (90) Colby and
his mother are not off by themselves. Play
that there are others around, and Colby
might be embarrassed by the scene.

*   In "Kale and Ice Cream" (pg 92) Tara has a
tiny window up in her door to talk through,
and the stool helps her be more bold than
she might have been. A bit sassy. Her re-
actions bring out the comedy. Go for it.

*   In "Money For Nothing" (94) our mom's
sass will help Stacy re-act; so mom, give it
to her. Stacy can re-act to the hiding place,
then the slobber.

"Kale and Ice Cream"

After a knock on the door, TARA pulls a stool up to the small latched window (peephole). She sees a MAN on the porch with a carton of juice bottles.

> MAN
>
> Hello young lady, is your mother home?

> TARA
>
> Maybe.

> MAN
>
> Maybe? You're not home alone are you?

> TARA
>
> I don't think that's any of your business. And I'm not supposed to talk to strangers. So goodbye.

> MAN
>
> Wait! I'm here to offer **your mother** a healthy food subscription that I think she'd be interested in. Our cleansing vegetable solutions help us stay fit and trim for only $4.99 per drink.

TARA

You want my mother to give you five
bucks for that bottle of green stuff?

MAN

It's made from kale and asparagus,
both super foods.

TARA

Yuck! I'm going to **super** barf just
hearing about it.
No. Thank. You. For five bucks we
can get a great big carton of ice
cream. The good kind!

She slams the little door and jumps off the
stool.

END

"Money For Nothing"

Mom is in the kitchen when Stacy rushes in.

STACY
Mom! I need money for tonight—
everybody is going to the Crab Shack
and I can't go with no money. And
dad said I have to earn it, but I don't
have time to work for it.   And he
won't just give it to me.

MOM
No, we earn our money around here.

STACY
He gives YOU money and you don't
work.

MOM
Ex-cuse me? You want to explain
that comment while I'm cooking or
while I'm doing the laundry?

STACY
That's not what I meant, I mean you
don't GO to work.
        (sees Mom's glare)
I mean … uh; this isn't going the way
I wanted.

MOM
I'm sure it isn't.

MOM (cont'd)
Tell you what: I'll loan you the
money if you can name three things I
do for you.

STACY
I didn't mean it like that. Ok, dinner,
laundry, chauffeur, homework, nurse
… I could name a dozen. Sorry.

MOM
Thank you.

STACY
I'll just come home after the game.

MOM
I didn't say you couldn't go. I just
thought a little appreciation would be
nice. There's a twenty in the dog toy.

STACY
Thanks, Mom. The dog toy? I do
appreciate you. Really.
        (grabs it)
Ew, yuck, slobber. Thanks.

She takes the $20 and runs out.

95

"Do or do not. There is no 'try'"

- Yoda

"Shorty" Scenes

Sometimes we get a part or an audition that isn't several pages long; it's only a few lines. We need to make those lines come to life in a short amount of time.
Let's practice.

"Target The Thief"

Two kids are shopping in Target when they see a man slip a watch into his pocket.

> **TRACY**
> Did you see that? That man over there.

> **SASHA**
> Did he just put that watch in his pocket?

> **TRACY**
> Yes, he's stealing it! Go tell the clerk.

> **SASHA**
> I'm not telling her, you go tell her.

> **TRACY**
> Sshh. He's looking at us. Be cool.

They freeze, big eyes; can't help but look, then maybe hide behind a shirt as they tiptoe away backwards. A good comic moment.

"Baby Birds"

MORGAN is looking out the window when AUTRY enters.

AUTRY
What are you looking at?

MORGAN
That bird. It keeps flying away and coming back. I think there's babies in the nest.

AUTRY
She must be the mama bird. Yeah, look --- little heads are popping up.

MORGAN
Looks like she's going to feed the babies ....

They watch as the mama bird regurgitates her food into the baby birds' mouths. Their faces contort into ...

AUTRY/MORGAN
Yecchh!

"I Think I See The Problem"

LANA and CARLY are eating lunch.

LANA
That new boy Carter is cute. I'm trying to get him to like me but it just isn't working.

CARLY
You have to spend some time with him, get to know him.

LANA
I am. I asked him to play basketball with me yesterday.

CARLY
Good, that's a start. How did it go?

LANA
He couldn't handle my moves. I beat him like a drum.

CARLY
I think I see the problem…

"Right In The Can"

Two bored friends are slumped in their chairs watching tv. One grabs some paper, wads it up, and nods to a distant trashcan.

DREW
Watch this. Right in the can.

Lou looks at the distance, back at Drew…

LOU
You're never going to make that.

DREW
Wanna bet?

LOU
I'll bet you a nickel.

DREW
A nickel!? Ok. A nickel.

Drew shoots. 3 results to choose from:

Drew **makes it** (victory dance, Lou pays up)
Drew **misses** (dance and payment reversed)
        or
Drew **misses badly**, scares the cat who jumps up, knocks over the lamp and breaks it. **They gasp, then run out.**

"'Study' With Elaine"

RORY and BAILEY are on their phones looking for something to do.

RORY
Hey, let's call Elaine and ask her to come with us.

BAILEY
Nah, her mom never lets her do anything that's fun. She's probably home studying math right now.

RORY
Yeah.
(pause)
Hey, maybe we could ask her to come over here and "study".

BAILEY
I don't want to st ... oh. Oh!
(smiles; gets it)
Yeah. "Study".

Devious smiles as they call her.

"Bloodsucker"

JAKE sees his little brother MILES with his arm out, waiting for a mosquito to land.

> MILES
>
> Come on, little 'squito, try and bite me. See what happens.

SMACK. He swats it just as it lands.

> JAKE
> (messing with him)
> You killed it? It didn't even bite you.

> MILES
>
> It was going to. It was going to suck my blood. I did the world a favor.

> JAKE
>
> What if he was a daddy-bug? You just made his kid an orphan. Nice going, killer.

Jake walks away. Miles looks at the smashed bug, frowns for a second, then ...

> MILES
>
> It was going to suck my blood!!
> (looks again at the bug)
> Sorry. Jeesh.

"Spider In A Box"

BRADY brings AJ into his room.

BRADY
Want to see something really cool?

AJ
Ok, what is it?

Brady pulls out a shoebox.

BRADY
I caught this spider. A big, hairy one.
You sure you want to see it?

AJ
I'm not afraid. Let's see it.

BRADY
Ok, not too close. Bum da da dum!

AJ cautiously looks in the box, then puts his
palms up, like "I don't see anything." Brady
looks into the now-empty box.

BRADY (cont'd)
Uh-oh...

"Higher Ground"

JULIAN is watching a video on his phone and laughing hysterically. SAGE, his sister, peers over his shoulder.

> SAGE
> Who's that?

> JULIAN
> He's an internet celebrity!

> SAGE
> Why? What does he do?

> JULIAN
> This!

> SAGE
> He falls flat on his face?

> JULIAN
> Yeah. Cool huh? He's my hero.

She leans in and watches some more. Pats him on the shoulder; as she **exits**...

> SAGE
> Set your sights a little higher.

> JULIAN
> Why? Whoa, hahahaha!

"Clever and Sneaky"

MORGAN is pacing, thinking…

MORGAN
Ok. We need someone clever,
smart, and just a little bit sneaky.

EVAN
Who can we get like that?

MORGAN
Me!

NOTE FROM THE COACH

In this brief bit, there are several ways to
say, "little bit". We can stretch it out, we
can make it sound like an old movie villain
etc.

All three adjectives can have their own spin.
And, there are many ways to say that one
little syllable "me". It can have cheerleader-
like enthusiasm!! Or you can think the rest
of your phrase: 'Me. *Duh.'*

Or, surprised that Erin didn't know:
Me .. *who did you think I was talking
about?'*

"Where's My Phone!"

Younger sibling CASEY is watching tv when the older sister EMMA rushes in.

EMMA

Have you seen my phone? I need it!
My friends are trying to contact me …
Where is that … I've been calling but
it's on 'vibrate'. WHERE IS MY
PHONE?!

Casey shrugs, Emma panics….

EMMA (cont'd)

Arrrgghh!

She rushes out. Casey picks up a magazine
to reveal a vibrating phone.

CASEY

(imitates a previous
conversation)

Emma, could you please share some
of your ice cream? We don't have
any more. *No, I will not. I will be a
stingy older sister.*

(looks at phone)

Hmmm. 8 text messages, 5 missed
calls. Busy, busy, busy.

(puts phone down)

Coulda shared, but ya didn't.

Acknowledgements

This book would not be possible without the kindness and support of my wife, **Denise Loveday-Kane**. She was not only patient and encouraging through the process, but since she's been a working actress for over two decades, she read and advised me on the material.

The great artist **Tom Cain** designed the book cover, front and back.

And a huge thank-you to my kids, **Makena** and **Austin**, who also proofed the book and advised me when *"kids don't say stuff like that anymore."* Makena is a senior at the Los Angeles County High School For The Arts and a regular on 'Teens React'. Austin is a high school student in Burbank and a working actor (Criminal Minds, Godless, Bizaardvark, Criminal Minds, CSI, etc).

And a special thanks to the folks who run On Your Mark Studios in Los Angeles – Brian and Cinda Scott, and Sam Hixon. Each scene was tested several times, on-camera, in one of their studios.

And big thanks to all of my acting students, past and present, who come into class every week with enthusiasm, talent, and a willingness to help the old coach with these scenes and monologues. Some of them are pictured on the cover and below.

Bo Kane's On-Camera Acting Class

Tiber, Marleigh, Xander, Marley, Jenna, Anastasia, Bo, Arianwhen, guest casting director, Aristotle, Sabine, Dylan, Eddie, Hannah Mae, Isaac, Scarlet, Sarah, and Lucas.

About The Author

As an actor, Bo Kane has worked in television shows such as How To Get Away With Murder, Colony, Criminal Minds, Castle, CSI: Miami, Dexter, 90210, Workaholics, Outlaw, FlashForward, Men Of A Certain Age, The Defenders, The Unit, and films such as The Ringer, Camouflage, and Man Of The House. He began his career in the 80's, working in such films as What's Love Got To Do With It, El Norte, Child's Play, The Phantom, and on JAG, Melrose Place, The X-Files, Arli$$, General Hospital, The Magnificent Seven, and many others.

As a writer, Bo is a former newspaper columnist, penning "Man's Eye View" for the Sun-Times News Group, and "Hollywood Hoosiers" for The Times.

Bo has also worked on farms, in steel mills, as a newscaster for CBS affiliates, and for the U.S. Congress. He was the Head Coach for the Special Olympic Equestrian Team in the San Fernando Valley for 15 years, and is a graduate of the University of Notre Dame.

Aside from his acting and writing career, Bo currently teaches kids' on-camera acting classes in Los Angeles.
He has also coached his own two kids in baseball and basketball, causing him to use way too many sports metaphors in his acting classes.

"I love working with kids. Their eyes are bright, their laughs are genuine, their energy boundless, and their world has endless possibility."

- Bo Kane

Also by Bo Kane -

"Acting Scenes and Monologues For Kids! Volume I"

&

"Acting Scenes and Monologues For Young Teens"

"Writing is what you do when you're ready, and acting is what you do when someone else is ready."

- Steve Martin

Proof

Made in the USA
Columbia, SC
18 August 2017